JUDGMENT IS

ALREADY HAPPENING

ISABEL PERTHRO

Acknowledgements

Here I have to thank my friend Philippe that encouraged me to start writing books, without his help and support, this book cannot come out. Once I started the process, I have realized that it is not that hard to do it, and I will keep writing and hopefully each book I will provide something to you my lovely readers. And I know that this is my mission to write and publish it for those who would like to listen and follow, and I sincerely hope that you can find the answers from my book or anything else you are looking for, and pass in to others.

And I have to thank my publishing company that provides me a great deal of helping me edit my book, without the help, it must be much harder for me to publish it, and the cooperation between me and my publishing team strengths my ideas of keeping writing, and I sincerely wish that you guys can enjoy it as we put much work on it.

And in the beginning of 2026, I wish that everyone who reads have a great and lovely year!

Kind Regards,

Isabel Perthro

Table of Contents

CHAPTER ONE

FINAL JUDGMENT

This term Judgement comes from the Bible is well-known, and different people have different opinions about Judgement and eschatology, especially Christian scholars. And I see some Christians really struggle here, so as a polytheist who is psychic, I do have some concerns about this, and hope my work can help each of you, no matter which background you are from.

Such as Augustine, who is a Christian influences Christian belief a lot, proposes that only people who are faithful into God will be saved into God's kingdom. However, it is not correct.

The judgement is based on people's behaviors rather than faiths. Even though you do not have any faiths or believes, you will not be judged and punished in this part. The judgement is only based on your daily life behaviors. And the judgement is already started, so correcting your behaviors and thoughts is important in order not to suffer from it. And do not think or believe that you can escape from the judgement, all the information is in your soul, you cannot lie to escape.

Then what's the standard of the judgement? Basically, anyone who does not do bad things or does not intentionally harm or hurt would pass the judgement. And you need to clear that going to jail due to crimes would not be counted to decrease or eliminate the sins so that can be escaped or mitigated from punishment in the process of judgement. The earthly or physical punishment in the would does not work afterlife. The deities will judge spiritually after you die according to what you did or have done. For example, you are adjudged to be the jail because you fraud someone, this part of your sin will still be fully judged afterlife and your atonement in the jail will not affect the final judgement. And if you have done something serious but escaped from lawful judgment, you will be punished double through your final judgement.

To be clear, you are okay just to be a normal person as long as you don't harm or hurt someone, you will be fine to pass the judgement as the exam. And people inevitably have negative, evil or harmful thoughts, and definitely it's hard to get zero of it, so it is rarely counted in the process of judgement, therefore, not letting your bad thoughts affect your behaviors so that harming or hurting someone is important and you may need to start to learn this lesson. It may have different standards for the groups of magicians or witches, we will discuss later in my other books. And of course, hiring or paying someone to do something bad will be counted into judgement as well.

CHAPTER TWO

THE PUNISHMENTS OR TORMENTS

This topic is frequently discussed, and different people have different opinions about it, so I will use my knowledges to explain to you what torments or punishments are,

Many religions have some descriptions on that, however, not every information is correct. First of all, there are three ways of punishments or torments. One is to keep reincarnation to experience something really bad or horrible in our current world, for example, you can be born as animals in the next several lives so that you can experience scenes of keeping being slaughtered, or you can definitely have different terrible experiences in your reincarnated lives. Another is to keep in the underworld of purgatory area to suffer torments according to your sins. Normally, the underworld does not only have purgatory area, it has residential area and others, which depend on whose territory or underworld. The last is to combine physical punishments and purgatory torments together, people can experience both for the sins.

CHAPTER THREE

REWARD

Some of you have done something really good, then you deserve to get rewarded. For example, some people are glad to help others, then this behavior will get praises like integrations, which brings you into different levels. And according to your points, you will have more freedom or choices to choose where you are going to stay. There are lots of worlds besides our three-dimensional world, and different worlds have different rules. And some of you may want to work for the deities, which is possible, as underworld works are many, so you may get one and live in the underworld. And some of you may have chances to live in the upper world which is normally called 'heaven', however, it is strictly selected. And for who has a faith or works with some deities, is more competitive with others under the same conditions. Same applies to the underworld works as well, someone who has a faith or works with that deity is more competitive under the same conditions. However, not every believer, magician, or witch is competitive, as I said, the judgement is based on what we have done or behaviors, if you have done something really bad, it means that you would not only lose the opportunity but also would get punishments or torments. See, it is just a bonus point, and it is not the way of escaping from the punishments or torments.

Some of you may wonder that if there is no way to escape the punishments or torments, then what is the meaning to do something good? To be clear, it is not hundred percent that your sins can be 'reduced' or eliminated, however, it actually works based on different situations. If a person has done something not that serious, what you have done something good such as donating to someone needed, and what you have done something good is way more than something bad you have done, you will definitely pass the judgement, so no need to worry about that. However, if you have done something really bad or serious, no matter how many good deeds you have done, you cannot escape the punishment, because deities know that the intention you do deeds is to escape the punishments, which it is not allowed. But the good deeds you do may give you a chance to choose which you would be punished from the options. Thus, starting to change right now would help you for the final judgement.

CHAPTER FOUR

THE PROCESS

Some of you may wonder the process of the judgement, then let me tell you you this. First of all, the death deities would travel through the world to guide the souls to the underworld. For our world, different areas have different death deities to do the work. For example, Hela does the job in North Europe, Chinese deities such as Heibai Wuchang do the work in China, and different deities rule different areas in North America. As you can see, it is normally according to the country or area's mythology to distribute tasks. However, it is not exactly working in that way. For example, if your faith is Taoism but you are not in China, you will still be guided by Chinese deities. But if you don't have any faith or don't believe in any deities, then you will be guided by that area's death deities. Then you may ask, what about you have several different beliefs, then what will be? Basically, it is which death deity is free then which one will guide your soul. Or if you have a really great relationship with a single deity, you will be guided by corresponding death deity or that one. Besides, what if a country or an area does not have a mythology of death deity, then what it will be? Basically, the deities will follow the principle of Proximity, which means whose work area is close to that place, then that deity will do the guide work. Therefore, once your souls arrive in the underworld, according to different situations, you will be sent to different places, and of course, some of you can choose by your own. For those who do not pass the judgement, you will be directly sent to suffer either in the underworld you arrive or the earth, or maybe your 'points' can let you choose to go to another deity's underworld to suffer, then you will be sent there. For those who pass the judgement and do not have any beliefs, you will be sent to another world to live rather than this earth, or some of you are good to qualify the jobs, then you will get the jobs to live in underworld or upper world. To be clear, it is according to whether there is an exception for hiring or the need for new employees. However, you can defiantly and simply just live in the underworld or upper world without working and just by the permission of that deity. This is because some of your ancestors have a job or simply live in the underworld or upper world, and they have enough 'capital' to get you there. Otherwise, you will be sent to another one of existing world. For those who pass the judgement and have a belief or have done some spiritual or magic practices, you can live with the deities with the agreement or permission, sometimes, deities will proactively contact the underworld which you do the exam so that you will be send directly to that deity's kingdom after you pass the judgement. But if there's more than one deity that giving you chance to live in their kingdom, you can choose which one you want to stay, it's a two-way selection. Some of you may do spiritual practices such as vampires, it definitely would strengthen your power, however, you still need to go through the judgement process, no choices to escape. Without passing the judgement, you still need to get punishments or torments. As you can see, there are lots of work in the underworld, the judgement, the choices, the sendings, each process requires works, so that's why it is easier to get hired for underworld jobs, and for those who are connected with or have a good relationship with death deities are easier than others to get hired.

CHAPTER FIVE

THE OLD WORLD? THE NEW WORLD?

As I have mentioned the underworld jobs, you may wonder what the heaven or upper world deities do, let me tell you right now. Deities who rule over the upper world are more responsible for managing, controlling, maintaining, repairing or even destroying the worlds if they find something wrong. As our world is just one of existing worlds, they do have affairs to work on the other worlds such as responding to prayers or upgrading the world's dimensions, therefore, you may also get a job. And they may just upgrade our world that reaches a higher dimension, which can be considered as new world, and some of you who pass the judgement will be sent there to live. This is one of solutions. And you may wonder what the old world will be? It finally will become a trial ground or purgatory for those who do not pass the judgment to suffer, and whether will be destroyed is totally decided by deities. If they feel that the people who failed the judgment are hopeless to change or get better, they will think to destroy.

CHAPTER SEVEN

WHO CREATES?

As I mention that the deities are responsible for upgrading dimensions and it will lead to a new world, which is kind of creations. Then you may wonder who creates the worlds? Honestly, it really depends, not all the worlds are created by them. To explain to you better, let me give you an example. Human beings created AI, and if there's a world where AI stays, then in AI's perspective, human beings are their creators and Deities. Do we or people who create AI are really Gods or Goddess? Absolutely not. However, the world is created by us no matter in a conscious or unconscious way, thus deities have to mange these worlds to keep all balanced. You need to be clear that deities they do have abilities to create worlds, but not all the worlds are created by them. And sometimes a creature is just created by another creature. In order to make sure the development of that world is working good, deities have to control it and they do have rights to interpret if needed. As I see, they are more supervisors.

Chapter Eight

Animals Cultivation?

Yes, some animals do have chances to cultivate or in our human understanding as spiritual practices, but the behaviors are still needed to be 'good'. Natural of eating other animals due to the needs is okay and fine, but absorbing human energy and essence is not okay. However, if a person really does something bad, it is okay to give him some punishments. For the judgment, they do not need to go to underworld to get the exam, as long as they feel it's time, they can ask for the test, once they pass the exam, they can be guided to travel to another world. The animals who are born as punishments (from final judgement) are not allowed to cultivate. I cannot provide every detail here as there are many, however, the deities they do know the standards, so there is nothing worrying for human beings.

CHAPTER NINE

LOCAL DEITIES?

Some local deities such as the deity who rules the land, can have a test any time, and once pass it, they will be allowed to live in another world. It is just another more comfortable place they live, and they can still work for the affairs even though they do not live in this world.

CHAPTER TEN

REVENGE?

Some revenges are considered not to be counted, however, it is not every revenge that can not be counted. I cannot give every detail of that, but mostly and generally, it is based on your experience that cannot obtain the justice which due to that, the revenge is considered not to be counted. For example, if a man kills a girl but he does not get lawful punishment, then her parents can punish him without or with less sins during the judgment, and it is not relative to lawful punishment. To be clear, even though it is less or not counted in the final judgment, people still need to be judged according to the laws, it does not mean that people do not have to go through lawful judgment. That's different, you have to be clear about that. Some people's the so-called revenge is not really a revenge, it is nothing more than something done under the guise of revenge. The deities can distinguish everything, and it would not work or not to be counted as every information is recorded, and you can not just use excuses or lie to the judge for you have done something wrong. You have to be clear about it and do not cheat yourself by using this excuse. And some people have to be clear that sometimes other people do not do anything wrong to you, and your revenge literally would be counted in the judgment if you have done this. For example, some people think that others should serve them as they are in a higher level of caste system such as Brahman, especially when they go to another country and think others shall treat them as Queen or King, and revenge people because the people of that country do not serve them, that's totally wrong. And your behaviors would be counted as sins, and you do not get any injustice from it, therefore, it is not a revenge, the things you have done is just to satisfy your own desires and treating it as your excuses. You would not pass the judgement, if you have this mindset and keep doing it.

Of course, if you have done something bad, it would also be recorded, and you can not use excuses or lie to the judge.

In the End

I cannot give every detail here that which behavior is considered to be good and which behavior is considered to be bad as every single person is an independent and special case, but generally, do not intentionally harm or want to get benefits of free is considered to be good enough to pass the exam. Of course, there are some other things can be considered as good and bad, but there are too many to say, therefore, trying to be kind and nice to people who are not bad and help others is the best way to do ourselves and pass the judgment.

If you really have some questions that want to get the answers, you can leave your questions to isabelperthro@gmail.com